THE HERMIT KINGDOM
POEMS OF THE KOREAN WAR

THE HERMIT KINGDOM
POEMS OF THE KOREAN WAR

Paul M. Edwards
Editor

Center for the Study of the Korean War

This edition was printed directly from camera-ready copy.

Copyright © 1995 by Center for the Study of the Korean War

ISBN 0-7872-0440-4

Printed in the United States of America
10   9   8   7   6   5   4   3   2   1

Contents

ix

Foreword

When the *Oxford Book of Modern Verse 1892 - 1935* was published it appeared without any poetry from World War I. The editor W. B. Yeats, himself a well established poet, felt the "passive suffering" reflected in such poems was not "a theme for poetry."[1] He rejected the contributions of this generation, as well, because he felt this poetry betrayed the nature of war, and the proper human response to it. "If war is necessary," he wrote, "or necessary in our time and place, it is best to forget its suffering, as we do the discomforts of fever, remembering our comfort at midnight when our temperature fell."[2]

Time has challenged both of Yeats' assumptions. Many of the poems of World War I have proven to be classics. And Americans, at least, have witnessed some very serious changes in both the acceptance of war poetry, and the understanding of war.

Historian Keith Robbins estimates that more than a million-and-a-half poems were written in August of 1914; that is 50,000 poems a day.[3] Can this possibly be true? While I do not know how such a count could be taken, the possibility reflects the role played by poetry in the early days of the War. At the turn of the century poetry was the language of patriotism, and at that time patriotism was the story being told. For war was seen in all its romanticism and was recognized as a holy struggle during which the most fundamental of truths became apparent. Generally, however, this early poetry was lacking in personal comment, and strangely "removed from immediate experience."[4]

Following the Battle of Somme in 1916, surely one of the most unnecessary and wasteful battles of all modern warfare, the poetry of World War I became more personal. It began to reflect the soldier's growing disillusionment with this senseless war of attrition. But, even under these conditions, it still managed to see the battlefield, as well as the war, in universal terms.

During World War II both the amount of poetry and the character of poetry changed. First, the number of poets decreased dramatically. Second, they did not speak in the grand gestures reflective of universal truths on, or off, the battlefield. Rather these poems are very personal. They reflect rage and anger, not so much against their war as against war in the abstract. Few poets of the Second World War reflect the inherent patriotism of earlier generations, but neither did they reflect the general and unfocused disbelief which is found in the poetry of later wars.

Skipping the Korean War for a moment, one quickly sees the anger expressed in the poetry of the Vietnam War. This poetry is full of rage and of despair which seems to arise from an utter disbelief in the events taking place. Lacking any respect for national interests, and often reflecting the outsider character of the authors, the poetry of this period is personal, immediate, self-directed, and lacking much of the abstraction traditionally found in poetry.

What then about Korea? Caught like a shadow between World War II and Vietnam it was a very different war, and one which reflected a transition in war poetry. Fought at a time and place where Americans did not want to fight, it was the first of the non-patriotic wars. A war during which participants expanded to an art form the idea that "getting it over" was more important that "getting it done." Not a patriotic war, it was

No subject for immortal verse—
That we who lived by honest dream
defend the bad against the worse.[5]

The Korean War broke out in June of 1950 when forces of the North Korean People's Army crossed the 38th Parallel to challenge the South. The "Hermit Kingdom" had been at war a long time before the Allies arrived to counteract the invasion. So, when on the evening of 25 July 1953, an armistice was finally signed, it promised a long absent peace for the land of the "morning calm." But peace never materialized. Not yet completed, the Korean War continues to demand preparedness, as it endangers our allies and kills our people.

It has been nearly half-a-century since the Korean War began and yet, as far as can be determined, this is the first collection of Korean War poetry to be published. Given the length of the war, and the intensity of the fighting, surprisingly little poetry appeared during, or since, the War. Some poets have commented that they could find no one interested in publishing Korean War poetry. Publishers, on the other hand, tell me no one sends them Korean War poetry.

Few poems from the War appear in the anthologies of the period. More incredibly, poems from the Korean War period are only rarely included in collections of war poetry. In Carolyn Forche's fine collection of poems about America's wars, *Against Forgetting: Twentieth-Century Poetry of Witness*, only one poet of the Korean period is included.[6] And his work is inserted in a long section dealing with the Vietnam War.

Many a veteran of this conflict feels the war is of no interest to anyone. They believe their responses, individual and immediate, are not as valid as similar reactions from other wars. Certainly their reflections of the war have few examples in American literature. The number of good Korean War novels could be counted on one's fingers.

Paradoxically the Korean War is often remembered in its forgotten state: the "unremembered" or "never known," "unreal" even "the ignored" war. Even now, as scholars are beginning to acknowledge the impact of the War, it is generally sub-titled to suggest a meaning: the "Korean Civil War" or the "Korean Revolution." The media, having some difficulty identifying it, first adopted Truman's phrase calling it "a police action;" the military referred to it as "a conflict" and only later did anyone finally acknowledge it was a war.

But it was an awful war. Whether you refer to veterans of the hard fighting of the early 1950s, those caught in the treaty violations during the mid-50s, or victims of one of the many flare-ups since the Armistice, the troops involved fought and are fighting a dirty war. More than a million persons have served in Korea. More than 150,000 American casualties have occurred. More than eight thousand men are still missing in action.

Unlike Vietnam the Korean War did not have the advantage of being a popularly unpopular war. A lack of focus, unidentified political aims, and limited military success, led to diminished American support. Service personnel questioned what they were doing and why, and got no answers. The home front hardly acknowledged the conflict. This distant war was not even considered important enough to hate. Rather the Korean War reflected a mediocrity of feelings; not passionately supported as was World War II, nor passionately confronted as was Vietnam. It was simply unpleasant, uninspiring, and unnecessary, and few desire to remember it at all.

Besides, the war never ended; there has never been a successful conclusion from which to look back and consider what happened. When the immediate costs got too high, and the political implications too dangerous, the more than thirty-five weary nations agreed they would no longer fight. But they did not agree on a peace. Today, at the 38th Parallel—in almost the same location where it began—the opposing forces face one another along a line known ironically as the Demilitarized Zone. Thousands of Americans have served as "fence walkers" along the southern border of the Zone.

The long days of boredom, the constant training, the daily anticipation of the renewal of combat, are sometimes more taxing than the battles. Monotony and danger—sporadic and premeditated—mark the passing days. The enemies are real, the battle still rages. Many Americans have been wounded during this forty year armistice; some have died.

In preparing this volume I did not encounter the problem reported by W. D. Ehrhart, the compiler of *Carrying the Darkness*, an excellent collection of Vietnam War poems.[7] The editor's greatest difficulty was in selecting between the hundreds of fine poems available. Rather, I have searched for the few good works available. Using modern computer aids, I searched a wide variety of publications; I contacted literary societies, newsletters, and journals; I sought the help of college and university creative writing, and English departments; I contacted veterans associations; and I networked through those poets who made their work available. And I have found some very fine works representing the war in its length.

Because the war never ended, and because fighting has broken out so often during the "peace," it is hard to define which are "war poems" as usually defined. The works collected here represent veterans of the hard fighting, persons who served in Korea at some time during the long armistice, or by persons who, having been affected by the long war, have chosen to reflect upon it.

And in the end I found a wide variety of poets, a deep and compassionate collection of poetry, and a sincere look at the War. While the majority of these poems have been previously published, a significant number appear here for the first time. Please note that author's poems have been printed just as they were originally published, or as made available by the authors.

In this effort I have had the help of many persons. A lot of these have works which appear in the volume. Others, editors, authors, friends, have made suggestions, collected materials, or searched for lost authors. In particular, I want to express my appreciation to Ashley Cunningham-Boothe of the British Korean Veterans Association, Jack Garnier for graphics, and to Joni Wilson of the Center for the Study of the Korean War. Her continued help, careful skills, and dedicated manner have been a major contribution to this book.

Endnotes

1. Robert Giddings, *The War Poets*, (New York: Orion Books, 1988) 6.

2. Ibid.

3. Keith Robbins, *The First World War*, quoted in Giddings, 8.

4. Giddings, 7.

5. C. Day Lewis in Michael Harrison and Christopher Stuart-Clark, *Peace and War: A Collection of Poems*, (New York: Oxford University Press, 1989) 84.

6. Carolyn Forche, *Against Forgetting: Twentieth-Century Poetry of Witness*, (New York: W. W. Norton & Company, 1993).

7. W. D. Ehrhart, *Carrying the Darkness*, (Lubbock, Texas: Texas Tech University, 1985).

Sources and Permissions

All poems appear by permission of the respective authors unless otherwise indicated here.

Rita Adams, **Casualty**, first appeared in *The Christian Century*, (August 8, 1951) 916. David Biespiel, **Lilacs**, Copyright (c) 1992 by The Antioch Review, Inc. First appeared in the *Antioch Review*, Vol. 50, No. 3, (Summer, 1992). Reprinted by permission of the Editors. Pauline Larimer Binford, **Home-Coming**, from Frances Parkinson Keyes, *A Treasury of Favorite Poems*, (New York: Hawthorn Books, Inc., 1963) 261. William Conelly, **November 11th**, first appeared in *The Epigrammatist* (Spring 1992); **Field Burial**, first appeared in *The Epigrammatist* (Spring 1993); **Oath of Service**, first appeared in *Drastic Measures* (Spring 1988). Ashley Cunningham-Boothe, **One Time Out of History's Calendar**, from *British Forces in the Korean War*, (United Kingdom: The British Korean Veterans Association, 1988) 158. Paul M. Edwards, **Soft Snow**, first appeared in *Hemlock*, (May 1959) 26. Reprinted by permission. John Jacob, **Monterey Language School**, first appeared in *Lakeside*. Ian E. Kaye, **Korea, 1951**, first appeared in *British Forces in the Korean War*, (United Kingdom: The British Korean Veterans Association, 1988) 155. Permission granted by Ashley Cunningham-Boothe. Peggy Menegakis, **She's A Nurse**, first appeared in *Greybeards*, vol. 7, no. 3, (April 1993). Patricia Monaghan, **Home Movies**, first appeared in *Call It Courage: Women Transcending Violence*, (Philadelphia: Temple University Press, 1993). Terry Moore, **The Land of the Morning Calm**, from *British Forces in the Korean War*, (United Kingdom: The British Korean Veterans Association, 1988) 159. Pat O'Connor, **Korea**, from John Melady, *Korea: Canada's Forgotten War*, (MacMillan of Canada, 1983) 143-144. Reprinted by permission of John Melady. Kathleen Patrick, **Silk Dragons**, first appeared in *Night Talk*, (1991). Harold L. Putnam, **Ghosts of War**, first appeared in *Greybeards*, vol. 7, no. 4 (June 1993). Elspeth Cameron Ritchie, **General Medical Officer, Camp Casey, Korea**, permission granted by *Military Medicine*, vol. 156, (October 1991) 580-581; **Jewelweed**, permission granted by *Military Medicine*, vol. 156, (January 1991) 50; and **Infantryman—the DMZ, Korea**, permission granted by *Military Medicine*, vol. 157, (May 1992) 274. Roy Scheele, **Playing at War**, (Part III of "Saturday Mornings in the Radio Years") reprinted with the author's permission from *Pointing Out the Sky* (Sandhills Press, 1985). William Wantling, **Korea, 1953**; **The Korean**; and **Without Laying Claim**, first appeared in *The Source*, (Paradise, California: Dustbooks, 1966). Reprinted with permission from Len Fulton, PO Box 100, Paradise, California, 95967. Keith Wilson, **Guerrilla Camp, Korea, 1952**, reprinted by permission of the author and Clark City Press. Copyright ° 1992 by Keith Wilson/All Rights Reserved. Denis J. Woods, **The Field of Crosses**, from *British Forces in the Korean War*, (United Kingdom, The British Korean Veterans Association, 1988) 159.

Poetry

Rita Adams

Rita Adams wrote this poem in response to a January 8, 1951 Reuters account of some of the many Korean children who cried out for help and comfort. It was published in The Christian Century.

Casualty

My son, killed in Korea, stood before
The judgment throne, his comrades crowded near.
But each man knew he must be judged alone.
He raised his eyes, yet could not see his Lord
For press of a multitude, and could not hear
Whether his name were called for the endless cries
Of the cold, dead children, who shivered, and blocked his view.
And he remembered them . . . weeds along the wayside ditches,
Whipped by icy winds, hungry, homeless outlaws
Raising tiny arms in everlasting hope, in true
Faith, *O Mary full of grace*, that an adult world
Would see to them, save them, food-find and warm-love them.
So they cried without ceasing, "Omonee, Omonee, Omonee!"
"Mother!" *Mother full of grace*! . . . And the trucks filled
With ammunition, valuable war materiel, and above them,
All drove by, not even on the other side.
And night came, and more gear and ammunition,
And some of the cries were stilled. But always there were others
New-lost, new-orphaned. And so the long, loud crying rode
The bitter night; and night after night without diminution.
In sleep he had heard it. All heard. "Omonee, Omonee!"

One lost, cold and hungry child -- and the whole realm
Moves heaven and earth to aid. A thousand bereft
But demonstrates the curious mathematics of compassion:
A thousand lost children are silenced to a statistic, a column
Of figures -- world's leaven -- on a long page, and left
Still hungry cold and desolate. The Lord have mercy . . .

British troops lay by their machine guns tonight and listened to the cries of thousands of lost children . . . . They tried hard not to look at little children at the roadside wailing "Omonee, Omonee" (Mother, Mother).

1

Tom C. Armstrong

Tom C. Armstrong, a Korean veteran, is a Nashville-based writer also working out of Los Angeles and New York. He has written for print, stage, film, television, and radio. His poetry has been published here and abroad. He is married to the writer Beverly Beard and they have two daughters, two cats, and a "ton of books."

menhunt

Shells.

Recon.

Our platoon seemed as in a snail's race
the plastron of a carapace
for all that's brave in war,
and base.

We came up empty.

Shells.

R. L. Barth

R. L. Barth is a veteran of the Vietnam War but wrote this epigram on Korea, based on his experience. Barth is reported as a man who writes, and knows poetry. He currently lives in Florence, Kentucky.

The Way It Was

A world of baseball cards, gloves, balls and bats
With heroes like Ted Williams, "The Splendid Splinter":
Who knew "in military" among stats
Could be defined by, say, a Chosin winter.

David Biespiel

David Biespiel is a contributor to journals, including <u>American Poetry Review</u>, <u>Antioch Review</u>, and the <u>Ohio Review</u>. His father, Lt. Commander (Ret.) Stephen E. Biespiel, served in Korea on the salvage tug <u>USS Current</u>. David has taught at the University of Maryland, Mount Vernon College, and Lynchburg College as the Richard H. Thornton Writer-in-Residence. He received the Wallace E. Stegner Fellow in Poetry at Stanford University.

Lilacs

—Allston, Massachusetts, 1985

Leeward of the house is nothing but the tip-
Tapered leaves and the sweet blooms' purple
And white pyramidal clusters. In the shade
The petals are dark as plums or thumb-sized
Knots of blackberries, though in the sun
They're gray as sea water almost rippling.
When she comes to pick them after school's out,
They lean, as if to weep, to her palm, a few
Sprigs falling to the concrete, the flesh of each

Touching as companions touch. She must know
They'll die, though it's summer she feels
In the smooth oval green when she cracks the stems.
Above her hair, which is straight and black,
Above the wide petals of the early evening
Primrose, right and left of the lilac bushes,
There are only waves of clouds that crumble,
Bulge, and subside. I don't think she cares
About the clouds. They bloom and fall.

more

4

David Biespiel

She's found a heaven to put in the window.
And I know she doesn't think of my father
At the salvage tug's anchor cable,
Near the Korea Strait's eastern channel.
It's 1951, the sky filled with a close knowledge
Of the gunfire's blue-red clusters of smoke.
He's at the winch, watching the hawser slacken
As it hooks in the damaged vessel.
Punctures the side of plums or blackberries.

Two men, to the right and the left
Of my father, will be shot. They will die.
Cut down, he'll say. Unlike the primrose
On each side of the lilacs. So dark,
The top ones beyond any reach or pull
But the wind's, and visible in the lamplight
Where the great clouds span like phantoms
Bearing blood, water, flower, sky.
Those things we never give up.
Be it late spring. Be it cloudy weather.

Pauline Larimer Binford

Pauline Larimer Binford's poem first appeared in the <u>New York Times</u>. Every effort to identify, or locate, her has proven unsuccessful.

Home-Coming

At first he had not wanted much to go,
To leave his mother and the kids alone;
Since Dad had died, they counted on him so,
As though at eighteen he were fully grown,
As for Korea -- just a pinkish blob
Upon the dime-store globe -- he'd never thought
He would be needed there to do a job.
He could not understand just why they fought.
And now his mother and the kids are there
Just where he left them in the crowded station.
A flag is draped, and someone says a prayer
And speaks about a posthumous citation.
His little brother pats a brave bronze star,
And wonders: "Is Korea so far?"

6

William R. Bowman, Sr.

William R. Bowman, Sr. was born in Kenosha, Wisconsin, and attended the University of Wisconsin on both an art and athletic scholarship. He trained with the 101st Airborne and was assigned to the Far East Command with the 586th QM Co., Military Police and rose to the rank of S/Sgt. He is an active artist, writer, illustrator, and inventor, and currently is with television production in Pensacola, Florida, and is President of the Pensacola Press Club.

Morning Crosses

You see them first from the approaching road
Like soft fallen snow or frost lying undisturbed
across the green rolling hills
awaiting the warmth of the morning sun.

Closer now, around the bend
and down a single row of stately elms
standing guard at parade rest
their long branches arching over your head.

The road carries you to the open plain
where star white crosses spread
and weave a fabric of endless shame
that covers our youth so recklessly spent.

I hear their voices, no longer far,
as my feet touch each morning star
that greets the new sun at this place
so filled with memories and empty face

And sunlight sparkles with crystal hue
as my footprints trail a wandering line
in parallel rhythms of marching steps
creating a long green stripe behind me.

I feel the first wave of warmth arise
like frightened calls between night and day
that echo from the earth below my feet—
a call for life and joyful play.

more

William R. Bowman, Sr.

My eyes travel through time to a place
so distant from this life we know
where mornings are wet with reddened dew
among the tangled vines and endless mud.

I hear the laughter of anxious boys
and smell the dampness of the morning sun
where sweat and waste and feces drain
in sunrise call for Mary Jane,
and hot coffee in steel cups burns your lips
and last weeks socs will never come clean,
and Sunday mornings are but a dream—
and jokes and songs are lost in silent nights
thousands of miles away from home.
Here now, I no longer feel alone.

Lying here, struck down by time and place,
these morning crosses honor their grace
and wander no more among the nights of fear,
but rest gently in our tender care
the human dream we proudly share.

I feel their presence below my feet
and wish them well, their journey we protect
And vow in silence, among our dead,
the path of war shall never again be tread.

Garry Michael Buff

Garry Michael Buff is originally from Rochester, New York. He is an attorney with a BA in English and an MBA in finance. He resides in Manhattan with his wife Merle. Currently employed by a Canadian bank in New York, he combines his love of poetry with a strong interest in American military history.

Chosin Ones

The silver wings cut
through the ice air
and we sit below
in the chipped carved earth.
Darkness hugs and swallows us
like a black cotton cloud
and all sight ceases to exist.
We carry no more weight
than a can of beans.
We seek no prize.
Yet death hits
with the same heat
from the same hell.
We struggle with the same fear
and burn in the same brutal ocean.
Frozen agonies grip our minds
and fill our bellies
like a soup of the dead.
Cold battles the darkness
in a clash of has-been palookas
peering out from the colorless world
above a Friday night bar.
Limited war
meet
the infinity of death.
I see this now
as my buddy loses his guts and
my world loses it's mind.

Donald A. Chase

Donald A. Chase served with the 89th Infantry Division during World War II, and with the 24th Infantry Division in Korea. He was wounded several times and sent home in June of 1951. He returned to Korea in November 1952, and took part in the Iron Triangle Area with the 3rd Infantry Division. Following his discharge he worked construction, drove race cars, and made parachute jumps. Now retired, he volunteers with the Disabled American Veterans, and writes poetry.

Unwanted Memories

Often when I sit alone, and twilight fills the sky
    I find myself recalling scenes, from other years gone by.
Memories of Korea, still clutter up my head
    Those dreary days and hellish nights, and my friends long dead.

The many hills we fought through, which never seemed to end
    And all the while the fear inside, of death, around the bend.
The clashes with the enemy, who sometimes fled away
    But, for every hill we won, someone had to pay.

Maybe one was lucky, when a bullet found an arm
    For a little while at least, you were safe from harm.
My mind recalls the weather, when diseases took their toll
    When frozen feet were common, from winters numbing cold.

The trench line with its bunkers, and grimy faces there
    Where if you were observant, you saw the burnt-out stare.
The pathway from the trenches, which led to no-man's land
    A torn and barren piece of ground, destroyed by human hand.

Always, there were those who fell, never to arise
    And to this day, I still can see, the shock in startled eyes.
These vivid pictures locked inside, although they do not show
    Never seem to leave my thoughts, no matter where I go.

Donald A. Chase

Reminiscence

We climbed the hill in silence,
    just listening to the sounds of war.
And each in his own way and manner,
    tried to get ready for what's now in store.

All heartbeats started to quicken,
    as we thought of what goes wrong.
When shells and bullets start to sing,
    their always deadly song.

And so we heard this song of death,
    for many a night and day.
And fortunate indeed, were those of us,
    who were able to walk away.

But the sights and scenes encountered,
    as the days and nights went by,
Live forever in your mind,
    and at odd times, still can make you cry.

Time will erase all wounds 'tis said,
    but sometimes that's not true.
For when the wounds are deep inside,
    they become a part of you.

Donald A. Chase

Darkness Brought Death

Each time the daylight faded, and darkness filled the sky,
the waiting would begin, for the night to hurry by.
Darkness was the time that the enemy chose to strike;
knowing eyes grew dim and weary as they strained to pierce the night.

There was little sound or movement and the weather took its toll.
Bodies ached and stiffened, from winter's bitter cold.
Hours slowly passed, all senses showed fatigue.
Endurance had its limits, with sleep the crying need.

Suddenly without warning, flames and thunder rock the scene.
Shells and bullets hit their targets, while the night was rent with screams.
Man-made moonbeams lit the sky; flares added their glow.
Shadows twisted and danced, like some weird picture show.

Chattering machine guns sang their deadly serenade.
Shrapnel whined and howled, from exploding hand grenades.
From frozen snow-filled holes, men would fight to stay alive.
Sadly, though some did see a sunrise, many others also died.

Darian A. Cobb

Darian A. Cobb was born and raised in the Midwest. He served in Korea with Hq and Hq Battery, DIVARTY, Seventh Infantry Division (Army) during the latter part of the War. Since the War he has been an author, librarian, poet, and teacher.

4th of July

How do you tell your children
why
you do not want to see the
fireworks
provided by the local Mall?

Remembering with more pleasure
than guilt
the great phosphorescent
blooms
sent by 105s arching
against the midnight
star.

Being

Little was disturbed
on his face, young and smooth,
looking eversomuch as
if he didn't mind at all
the small brown hole
where his hair line arched
and his being lived.

more

Darian A. Cobb

The Poet

Somehow Robert Bly,
Naval hero and war protester,
Poet and man's man,
missed a whole generation
of death, and remains silent
against the conflict in
Korea. Did calling
his war unjust,
make ours holy?

Who Sent Us Forth, Who Made Us Go?

My brother died.
So simple was the act
no one recalled it happening.
But he was dead
none-the-less

News

When I was in school
        learning about life
I did not understand
        about time and space,

Until pieces of an old tin roof
        as big as the hands of
God, demanded the space
        where your chest had been.

Jim Cody

Jim Cody is a poet, essayist, a writer of fiction, and registered nurse. He taught English at Danguk University, Seoul, Korea, where he composed this poem. He is the author of Colorado River, Return, A Book of Wonders. He lives in the Northern Chihuahua desert.

Today

Yesterday Katie and John and Charlotte and I
drove out to Jin Gwan Sa,
12th Century Buddhist temple
before Katie's departure,
to show her a little Korean countryside,

to the steady rhythm of the nuns' prayers
punctuated by a novice's mok tak,
the hills echoing
      with howitzers,
      automatic rifles
      and shocked earth.

"No, the North is not invading,"
I reassure Katie,
"the South is only practicing."

But you never know,
here at the front lines
      between Marx and Malthus,
      Jefferson and Stalin.

more

Jim Cody

If not here,
they practice elsewhere,
constantly shifting position.
No countryside,
only twenty miles south of the DMZ,
is exempt,
nor, indeed, is all Korea.

But it's ok;
we understand.

In this century,
the monotonous Buddhist quest
for peace
is more appropriate than ever,
and I imagine that,
in the future,
the sound of automatic rifles
will be part of the ritual.

William Conelly

William Conelly grew up listening to war stories from his father who served with a bomber crew in Europe. After his father was called back into service in Korea, William Conelly joined the Air Force. He resigned his commission in 1964, and completed his Masters at the University of California. He has published poetry in the United States and in Great Britain and is currently at work on a manuscript titled Hill and Vista.

Oath of Service

Swear to maintain your motor skill;
Swear to resist and yet obey,
Till barring all you think or say,
You can enact your captain's will.

Swear righteously that you'll accept,
In forfeiture of blood and breath,
Your friend's as well as your own death,
So long as that one will is kept;

Know certainly, for all you care
Of politics or common fate,
You are the lowest gear of State,
Engaged and run by what you swear.

William Conelly

The Sniper's Mark

It's satisfying to betray
 So little feeling
To the corrugated ceiling
As you breathe haphazardly
Against your splintered ribs.

Somehow this makes you better
 This restrained acceptance
Of the slowly funneled distance
Eye to ceiling and beyond,
the ivory winter sky;

So draw your grating breath across
 Dry lips and tongue
With wistful courage, being young,
Before you faint through clouded fields
Of marigold and rose.

You will survive death's brutish kiss
 Much as before,
A puzzled afterthought to war,
Housed at the Y on pension checks
You tipple through or smoke,

Explaining at reunions
 In a flushed display
Of words and gestures strangely gay,
Your presence at that window ledge
That moment of that day.

William Conelly

November 11th

I notice fallen oak leaf clusters
Curl like the fingers of dead soldiers.

Field Burial

Place half dollars on his eyes.
He always longed for silver skies.

Ashley Cunningham-Boothe

Ashley Cunningham-Boothe, who served three active duty tours during World War II, the Korean War, and Malaya, is a published author, poet, editor, and lecturer. He was the first National chairman of the British Korean Veterans Association. He is publishing a joint anthology of poems and short stories with Ian E. Kaye entitled The Youth-an'Asia of Kaye and Cunningham-Boothe.

One Time Out of History's Calendar

I had slept, not long, the soldier's fractured sleep,
That parked its arse upon the razor's edge of my taut nerves.
Dawn was not yet in the making in God's black opal eye.
Night coalesced the sky with the uncharitable earth and the
Inhospitable mountains,
Making one great, dreadful black of darkness.

Then, from my raw-ragged sleep, to stark-naked awakeness —
Mortar bombs ripped vulgar clutches from the earth's bone-dry crust,
And arms and legs — I wondered who had "bought it,"
in my instant-packaged hell,
As all around me cries of wounded Fusiliers gnawed
away at the edges of my sanity.

Peering out of the sparse sanctury of my hole's inside:
My eye travelled along snatches of tracers,
Busy sewing seams along the edges of the night's darkness,
Looking for a carcass to bury their bright lights in.

And flares which, in a grim imitation of illuminated revelling,
Mushroomed their brightness into the great, black cavern of the night;
Punctuated by gregarious, rattle-tattle sounds that battles
make about themselves.

Screaming, whistling, bugle-playing, Banzai-yelling 'Gooks' —
Like raving lunatics doing a demented Morris dance —
Reminding me of fireflies on a balmy summer's night,
Thrashed the obscene loops and strands of barbed-wire ignominy;
Halting long enough to be stilled by the Fusiliers Brens and Vickers.

more

Ashley Cunningham-Boothe

Yet, still more came, and the more you shoot the Chinese,
The more there seems to be to shoot,
In a never-ending parody of insanely stupid, terribly worthless,
Quite courageous acts of raw courage.
Or was it opium, we asked?

When it comes to courage, which of you can separate the stupid
from the brave?
How can we take away from one soldier —
Because he serves the other side —
That which we would see as being nothing less than heroic in our own;
In battles so intense and infamous as to earn themselves a place in history,
Joining Battle Honours on a Regiment's Colours.

God forbid that you should spend one day of your life with the
'Shitdiggers' of the Infantry, writing history!

Lynne Hugo deCourcy

Lynne Hugo deCourcy is the daughter of a retired army colonel. A poet and essayist, she is the author of __The Time Change__ (Ampersand Press) and of __A Progress of Miracles__ (San Diego Poets Press). This poem is written in the voice of her husband's uncle, Lt. Colonel (then Major) Henry W. Seeley USMC (retired) who escaped, with the men under his command, from the Chosin Reservoir.

The Lieutenant

I'd chosen him
to go in my place
and he was pleased to; the supply plane run
was the leaving-dream seen
open-eyed, miseries diminishing
below,
       forgettable.
By then I'd had the unit
a good six months, made the trip
at least forty times, always claiming
for myself that expanse of time, white
noise insuring wordlessness
in recurring fields of sky.
               It bothers me still,
though I never believed a meaning
beyond the vagaries of chance. I know this much:
you can squint into blank horizons
while years turn your eyes milky
blind as what disappears
though no enemy has been sighted.
Squint and scan forever for something
invisible as the sheer of the wind
when it swallows;
           you'll never see a thing,
or hear more than what goes on
and on: the engine
coughing *Kyrie, Kyrie*, starting up
then humming *eleison,*
eleison rising and rising in your mind
toward an immaculate altitude.

Paul M. Edwards

Paul M. Edwards, educated as a historian, is the author of several books on the Korean War, the latest Inchon Landing: Korea, 1950. He served with the 31st Field Artillery in Korea and is currently executive director of the Center for the Study of the Korean War in Independence, Missouri.

Morning

Each morning I
lie to myself
just to rise from bed,
pretending I am
whole
no longer gut shot
with fear
nor left bleeding
and ignored on
a stranger's field of
battle.
Telling everyone who
will listen,
I am the same contented
young man
who lay down to sleep
just forty years
ago.

Paul M. Edwards

Sad

What's wrong, she asked
Are you okay? Of course
I said. Who can explain
that even the sun, lingering
behind a distant hill,
recalls death
in the early eve.

Corporal Red Harrington

I sought your name among
those carved into black stone
seeing my face reflected as I looked.
You were not there.
Does that mean you did not die?
Or was I mistaken about the war,
looking where only others
are remembered?

Paul M. Edwards

Soft Snow

Soft snow falls like magic dust
      upon the ravaged land
Hiding from view the blemishes
      of now dormant violence
And writing a fraudulent epitaph of war
      upon the souls of men
Who wait in expectation
      of distant thunder.

In spring the natural bloom
      and greenage bring a foil
to press the bunkers, pits,
      and graves in peace.
But still these aftermaths
      of war and death
Are etched in stark reality
      for all to see.

In fall the hail of rusted leaves
      mat down upon the earth,
And build and hide the shapes
      of violent scars.
But leaves blend too well
      with the stains of fallen men
And those who know, still see
      that the battlements of death remain.

But comes the snow, that might but tinge
      the earth with white,
And death and fear diminish,
      and hope appears
For dreams of cleanliness and peace
      and brotherhood of men.
One can not see the battlements
      of death remain.

Margaret Flanagan Eicher

Margaret Flanagan Eicher lives in Saratoga Springs, New York, and is the author of many published poems, including the forthcoming "Going Miles to a Funeral" and "Death of a Brother" accepted for <u>Death of a Sister or Brother</u>.

Roger

Sometimes when he's home
on leave from the hospital
he stands in the bathroom doorway
just holding his razor after he shaves,
his eyes wide
staring at her.

He shaves his psyche daily too
but it always comes out bristly.
War doesn't ruin only men's lives;
and war-ravaged women
do not suffer
only because of dead men.

D. J. Fitzgerald

D. J. Fitzgerald served with the First Marine Division during the Korean War and currently lives in Lake George, New York.

Sniper

To translate the colors into poetry;
To escape a gray and gibbering insanity. . .
these ideas I must fix firm
As dark figures move across the distant snow
Like ants of death within the mind—
And force a chance on Fate, in kind
To prosper yet amid the blind
and feckless graspings of an empty land.
My spotter says: "You got him."

Lynn Harper

Lynn Harper returned to the classroom after retirement, to pursue the craft of writing. Her works have appeared in several magazines, and small press publications both in the United States and Canada. She currently lives in Thousand Oaks, California, with her family.

Nightingale

My hand is the last one he holds
My face the last one he sees
"Don't go yet. . .he pleads
. . .until I leave?"

The mask of pain he wears
Fever shining in knowing eyes
Exploding shells. . .
Flames of hell. . .
Are torturing him inside
Red fingers clutching. . .
I can't let go

Not another one, I pray
Screaming silently. . .
This can't be so
How many can I lose each day?
Warriors. . .all so young
Merely boys
Are there quotas He must fill?

My powers useless
Tears of joy
Hours. . .
Minutes. . .
He's finally still

Lynn Harper

Parade Passing By

Laughing boy with a
Catchy grin
Hot dog stand in the park
Marching band on a
Lemon bright day

Her heart fails a beat
As the flag waves by
Plaintive strains
Of an old love song. . .

What melody does she hear
Again and again
When eyes scald with tears
Remembering, watching
The man in the shell

The shell of her man?

Lynn Harper

Snow Deep in Tears

"Walk proud, walk straight
walk tall," They said
Let your mind race with the
red, white and blue winds . . .

Hate! Kill your enemies!

In restless dreams
I call out long ago buried names
Waking, I try not to recall

For two score years and more
I have known not Peace
only War. I bled when
They said, "To die is glorious!"

They lied!

Richard Hill

Richard Hill has published poetry, fiction, and essays in <u>Georgia Review</u>,
<u>American Speech</u>, and <u>Southwestern Review</u>. He took his MFA from the
Iowa Writer's Workshop and currently directs the creative writing program
at Taylor University. He lives in Upland, Indiana, with his wife and son.

Reverie in the Nakashima America® Middle-Management Lunchroom

After Korea I came to Cal State for
an engineering course on the GI bill;
lived in off- (way off) campus housing, the poor-
married's quonset huts way out past Cow-Chip Hill.

I had a '40 Chevy panel straight-six
and a Japanese wife. For a class one time
I chopped the Chevy's roof clean-off and fixed
a hydraulic ragtop my prof called "sublime,"

and *Hot Rod* mag bought pix the wife's brother took.
Riding Sundays, me, Kiro, all her brothers:
three right-off-the-boat cheap-suited little cooks
in round steel specs reflecting one another's

smug glances when the damn top stuck halfway down
(it always did). I'd be cussing and sweating
at it while they whispered in Okinowan;
Kiro smiling, nervous; then me forgetting

my manners, making monkey and A-bomb jokes.
We'd finally get rolling out by the pig
farms and chicken ranches. They never once spoke
to me direct; they'd just nod and grip those big

briefcases they always carried. Come late fall
and the storms, I had to wrestle the ragtop
back up, sweating midterms, trying to recall
all those damn trig formulas while fat raindrops

more

Richard Hill

sizzled and heat lightning reflected in those
six little lenses. Thirty-some years it's been
but I can still see them, smell their wet wool clothes
just as plain as I could feel Kiro's wet skin

in a hot bath when we'd get home, after I
dropped the three sopping brother-sans at their loft
over the Chinese Restaurant . . . And she'd sigh—
Oh Hell, here I go again—she was so soft—

both of us in that old clawfoot tub, spoon style,
her small chest against my back, and she's teaching
me Jap words for ear and lips, for kiss and smile;
and me all misty-eyed, then warm, then reaching—

Meanwhile, her brothers—those soggy-suit slant-eyes—
would be sneaking back, pulling out rulers, pens,
flashlights from those briefcases—those little spies,
they copied my hydraulic system and then

built one for themselves on a '34 Olds
they'd jury-rigged together. And the next time
we're out by ourselves, here they come—all with colds,
but grinning—the Olds clanking up from behind,

its top rising up, slick as on a new Cad;
and they're waving, their specs are glinting away:
enough to make an easy-going guy mad—
though it's almost funny, sitting here today.

All three brothers cooked their way through M.I.T.
and I didn't see much of them till Kiro's
funeral—she got cancer in '63—
And all I said to them was, "You so-and-so's—"

(never can remember those funny first names)
"I would've given you those blueprints for free—"
(they wore silk suits and shades with designer frames,
and they grinned) "all you had to do was ask me."

32

Mark Hillringhouse

*Mark Hillringhouse was Poetry Director for the William Carlos Williams
Center for the Arts in Rutherford, New Jersey, and has worked as an
editor for both the <u>New York Arts Journal</u> and the <u>American Book
Review</u>. He was the winner of the Eerdman's Poetry Award in 1979, and
the 1988 Passages North Poetry Competition. Currently he is American
editor for JSC Publications in England and teaches creative writing at
Passaic County College.*

1953

The mood was communism
and Boogie Woogie—
the year of the Polio Vaccine
and the space monkey.
Ted Williams at 35 was batting .407
in Boston just back from Korea.
It was the year Jersey Joe Walcott
sat down lost in thought in the first round
until counted out,
the way I'm sitting now
in the Short Stop Diner
thinking about my life between
the Garden State Parkway
and a Texaco station.
I was one of four million new faces
to appear on the planet, the year
Invaders from Mars landed in our backyards and
Alfred E. Butts invented Scrabble
and a new Zeeland beekeeper
climbed the world's tallest mountain.
The year Stalin died and the hottest thing on tv
was "I Love Lucy".
and I'm thinking now of Burt Lancaster
embracing Deborah Kerr on the beach
in the surf, "From Here to Eternity"—
making love for America.
I could have been conceived in that picture
only to surface out of my own dark surf—
warm and wet and naked.

Maureen Hurley

Maureen Hurley is a visual artist, photo-journalist, and poet. She lives near the Russian River where she is regional coordinator for California Poets in the Schools, and director of <u>Poetry Across Frontiers: Sonoma Heritage</u>. She has published in <u>The Louisville Review</u>, <u>American Poetry Review</u>, and won a <u>San Francisco Bay Guardian</u> poetry award for the "Sixth of August" in 1987.

Sixth of August

The personality of the dead woman in the storage room escapes
from boxes of silk scarves, photographs, letters
cellulose toys, yellow mother of pearl buttons and cloth scraps.
Inside her white plastic purse;
a checkbook, unclaimed raffle tickets,
a tiny snapshot of a girl who still sends her love;
an envelope dated 1937,
some eight cent stamps and a life insurance policy.

On this 40th anniversary of Light,
I pull stamps of Einstein and Eisenhower apart.
Glued on top of a glib Eisenhauer grinning seven times
a haunted Einstein broods in purple; the color of mourning.
Beneath them, postage stamps of Apollo on the moon,
black-wreathed earth against the sun;
the birth of Man in space.

When I was three, the linoleum to cover the stairs
was put in the storage room to change it from green to red,
my uncle told me. And so it did.
I admired the miracles that happened in darkness.
In that same darkness, copper pennies
dropped into the piggybank turned into steel.
Dressed in khaki-green, my uncle tossed me into the air
and the known world spun past my forehead.
He held a suitcase of darkness in his hand.

more

Maureen Hurley

Now, I've gone and brought the dead woman's things into light.
A photograph of her husband holding a silver-plated trophy
by the tall grey horse at Longacre track:
He stares at me with such frankness, that with his passing
I feel the loss of an intimate stranger.
The bent and tarnished trophy rests in thick dust.

When I wear the clothing of the dead,
they see glimpses of light again.
The poet's shirt gives me strange dreams
but I forget the words by morning.

Rotted with age, the boxes of yarn
in this half-light makes tufts like the manes
of cloth horses I ride in my dreams
where the landscape grows wilder with each visit.

Maureen Hurley

Tocaloma Road*

The round sound of Tocaloma rolls off the tongue
like night drowning in the gibbous moon.
The herefords stop grazing and low to each other
as I help my neighbor gather topsoil for her lawns. *Tocaloma.*

We stop afterwards at the Western Saloon.
I sip sasparilla as she rolls down another beer
beneath the cobwebbed mooseheads.
At the other end of the bar, a gaggle of men
bang down a cup of Liar's Dice for another round.

Ranchers in overalls and gumboots
argue over what's the best feed for cattle. It's a lean year.
Two-wire bales of alfalfa sell at the price of three-wire bales.
We overhear them talk of planes dropping emergency feed
to livestock stranded on the open ranges.
Toby's Feed is shipping in the last of the Nevada hay.
I'm having trouble feeding my horse.

The corners of Agnes's mouth turn downward when she sips bourbon—
as if it were an uncertain pleasure.
She salutes the empty morning air, saying, *Sköl pifiskin*,
and I look for the *toofta* from Norway who always steals her drinks.

When her husband is at sea, and alcohol loosens inhibitions,
she tells strangers met in bars we have no socks.
Their eyes fill with easy tears, and during whiskey runs,
they take us to the General Store, buying me more white socks
than I know what to do with.

Tocaloma. To touch the earth.
The McIssacs went from milk cows to beef.
Alan says they couldn't make it any other way.
In the barn, we step over a dead weaner calf. He says, *Don't look.*
Their ranch stretches from the sky to the old Tocaloma train station.
Alan has a "stop" sign in his bedroom, but the cattle erode the hills
and fine silt settles in Papermill Creek. No good for salmon.

more

Maureen Hurley

On Sundays, her husband sends tightly written letters
on thin blue airmail tissue from Bombay, Hong Kong, the Mekong Delta.
Once, they hit his ship, loaded with ammunition;
we watched news images of the foundered "Baton Rouge" again and again.
It was several tense weeks before she heard he was alive.
I played with leopard cowries from the Indian Ocean,
and caucasian silk dolls with Japanese eyes.
My music box chimed *Sayonara*, filled with foreign coins
as she showed me on the big map where the stamps and letters came from.
On Sunday evenings, we'd listen to "Hawaii Calls" on the radio.

When the liquor warmed her blood,
she'd spend hours rolling white bread into little doughballs.
After they got good and gray, she fed them to Smoky, the springer spaniel.
She made me feel unclean for becoming a woman
as if it were something I could control—like those doughballs.
It was O. K. when we were still kids playing in the thistles.

My neighbor died in summer, when the waves turned golden,
and the lawn stretched to the hills like a green wave.
We pulled weeds, stood under sprinkler rainbows,
tumbled on the grass, until sky and land blurred, became one.
The rich black soil from Tocaloma sprouted healthy thistles
nourished by the cow paddies we stuffed into empty feed sacks.

Her husband drinks and thinks about the sea: *Korea. Vietnam.*
He planted the disease in deep so she never had children (other than us).
Couldn't, said Gram'ma, tisk-tisking.
Her insides blackened. The surgeon trimmed what he could,
but it wasn't enough. I felt nothing when I heard the news—

as if she were never there. And only now, twenty years later,
I am remembering all those lawns, and *Tocaloma—*
this place where we touched the earth
because the rolling hills and grazing cattle
weren't enough to feed the eye.

* for Alan McIssac

37

John Jacob

John Jacob has been an intelligence analyst, fund raiser, grant writer, social worker, and now teaches at North Central College and Northwestern University. His first novel, the Vietnam book Long Ride Back, won a PEN Discovery Award.

Monterey Language School

He went away to become a translator,
and intelligence grunt, to California
and the school where you spoke
languages you had never heard before
twenty hours a day. You got used to
not looking outside because it rained
every day, and before six months were
over they had pulled Jablonski down from
his own noose and cleaned up after Smith's
pistol to the mouth.

When you went overseas you drank
to spend the time and played cards,
stationed directly across a ravine
from a North Korean advance post.
You'd shove the binoculars to your
face and look into the hard blackened
eyes of the enemy. A mortar blew your
jeep off the road and your men spilled
like chess pieces when the board is
yanked away hard. You only lost one,
that time.

When you came back you sat in the
dark and when someone asked you to
speak North Korean, or Chinese, you
would do it in your head while saying,
"I forgot all that over there."

John Jacob

Reflected

Vapor trail in water
of all wars. The Captain
says "imagine every step
you take you are walking
on a real parallel and
a million Chinese are
coming over the next hill."

We named them well: Pork
Chop, # 609, in codes we
hoped would not be broken.

I remember sitting in the
cold shade of winter
kicking down a drink and
notching dum-dums into
my bullets.
Across the way, we heard
fire and we ignored it.

Uncle Bill came back with
shrapnel and no appetite.
He died at 47, drinking one
quart of beer a day, eating
one meal, smoking many
cigarettes. He was never right
after 1953.

The condensation on his
glasses
made him crazy: he suddenly
couldn't see, none of us
could see.

Ian E. Kaye

Ian E. Kaye, an Englishman, served for seventeen years with The Black Watch (The Royal Highland Regiment) and five years with the Argyll and Sutherland Highlanders during World War II and the Korean War. The best known British Korean War poet he published two anthologies: <u>Pick and Shovel Poems</u> and <u>Scallywag Poems</u>. He died in June of 1993.

Korea, 1951

Where the mighty ragged mountains
Rip the guts out of the sky,
And the desolation chills you
To the marrow of your bones.
Where the blinding drifting blizzards
Sear the unprotected eye,
And the biting bitter wind
Across the Yalu River moans.
A wild and savage landscape,
With its valleys grim and dreary . . .
Crag on wolfish crag, piled up, and
Glittering with the snows.
A harsh and brutal kingdom,
That would make an angel weary . . .
But your Scottish Soldier fought there,
And he knows . . . my God, he knows!

Susan Kelly-DeWitt

Susan Kelly-DeWitt is a freelance writer, teacher, and poet. Her poetry has appeared in Poetry, New Letters, Prairie Schooner, and Nimrod among others. In 1989 she received a Wallace Stegner Fellowship in poetry from Stanford University. Currently she is co-director of an arts empowerment program for homeless and low-income women.

Korea

1952: Guilt replays
a newsreel's flickering
trumpet of light:

A scrawny girl, so hungry, so hungry,
she rifles trash and eats
glass.

Her frantic fingers forage
a jagged mouthful, a mouthful of pain
to fill her belly.

Every afternoon, at Sacred
Heart Academy, we say a rosary
for the starving children.

Sister Philomena prays with us, onyx
rosary beads cinched around her
ample waist—

oh, those glittering black buds
of salvation . . .

James E. Magner, Jr.

James E. Magner, Jr. Professor of English at John Carroll University in Ohio, served as an infantryman with the headquarters company of the 1st Battalion, 7th Regiment, 3rd Division. In February, 1951, he was wounded by machine gun fire in North Suwon. He has published with The Golden Quill Press and Ryder Press.

Repository

"Be one on whom nothing is lost"

A reader asked
The Sportsline
what college quarterback
named Adam
died
in The Korean War.
No record.
Even from the army and alma mater.

I remember an evening,
lit by lantern of a tent
in Jimungi of Kyushu,
before we sailed from Sasebo,
a second in silence
thirty-two years ago
in hills above Beppu
(strange, that I retain the face
of a man I never knew;
perhaps, in the secret of things,
a gift of him to you.)

more

James E. Magner, Jr.

I remember
a tall dark quick body,
alert dark-eyed gaze
(How can I see, now, so clearly!)
above his golden bars
caught in lantern
and the shadows
of what was to be
his austered and steely way
to memory.

Impossible to mind, impossible to heart
that one so quick,
who stepped so quick
in pocket
and rifled passes forty yards
for alma mater and the infantry
could die
and be forgotten
(even by his academy)
by all except me
who see
his face still,
dark eyes, dark hair — dark God
who disappeared
with him.
(How does heart, do eyes remember?)

Vanesca!
(Do I spell his name correctly?)
Vanesca!
(I say it again, so someone will remember.)
Vanesca!
(What is this repository that keeps the names,
the souls of men!)

43

James E. Magner, Jr.

Zero Minus One Minute

The dawn has come
to sleepless night
again
and it is time for us to answer
from the gray, crystal holes
that seem to womb
just northern night and nothingness;
but we are there;
our eyes electric,
our bodies splinters
in bundled rags;
we are there
and we shall creak
our frozen bones
upon that crystal mount
that looms in silence
and amaze the world.

There is no sound
and the world doubts
that we exist
      in will
— that we will creak
like brittle crabs
upon that skull,
consummate mount,
into the very hollow of its eyes
that will flash us death
or simply stare us life
and frozen day
again.

James E. Magner, Jr.

To A Chinaman, In A Hole, Long Ago

Does that long-alone matron dream
that this, her bed-warm love,
so sleeps—self-graved, ice-wombed
amid the corn-stalk stubble
of the appalling distance
on the frozen face of day?
O father of your people
in some smoking hut in China
in which hunch the moon-faced children
of your still-now steely dreams,
I, your ordered searcher
with a killer on my sling,
do bequeath my life to you
that you might fly the Yellow Sea
to your startled matron's arms
and curl beholden
amid the pygmies of your loins.
But marbled you lie
—and I, somewhat alive—
this rock-white silent day
of our demagogue damnation.

Peggy Menegakis

Peggy Menegakis lives in Shrewsbury, Massachusetts, and lists herself as an "ordinary person" who feels deeply about the war. Currently she is involved in the POW/MIA issue including those of the Korean War.

She's A Nurse

SHE'S A NURSE.
NOT A WARRIOR.
YOU WHO WALKED THE LINE
KNEW HER BEST.
SHE SAVED YOUR BLOOD
FROM SPILLING INTO THE EARTH.
HELD YOUR LIMBS
FROM THE DUST AND THE SAW.
CHASED YOUR PAIN
WITH HER HEART
AND HER TOUCH
AND CRADLED YOU
FROM DEATH.

Patricia Monaghan

Patricia Monaghan is poetry reviewer for <u>Booklist</u> and the author of two volumes of poetry, <u>Winterburning</u> (Fireweed Press, 1991) and <u>Seasons of The Witch</u> (Delphi Press, 1992); and editor of two anthologies <u>Unlacing: Ten Irish-American Women Poets</u> (Fireweed Press, 1985) and <u>Hard Gifts</u> (New Rivers Press, 1993). Her father flew Mosquitos during the Korean War.

Home Movies

A Japanese meal has been made,
and sake brought and warmed, and
the kids dressed up in kimonos.

The conversation has been
instructive, for the children,
and somewhat baudy, for the rest.

At least one mention has been made
of Panmunjong. Then there was
a bilingual dirty song or two.

The daughters now bring out
the wood dolls from Japan and show
how the elaborately dressed hair

can be removed, leaving the head
momentarily bald while another
wig is brought from the case.

As the children grow sleepy
a sheet is tacked against the wall
and the projector brought out.

more

Patricia Monaghan

There is a little game to play
with the sake cups, so that
everyone is drunk by the time

the movies begin. Aerial views
of Korean fields, paddies, blue
distant hills. Smoke and flame,

real war movies. The men drink
and retell the squadron jokes
while the women clear and clean.

The children, holding their dolls,
watch the silent bombs land
on the bed sheet, over and over.

Patricia Monaghan

Dream Lives

I am a child hiding in bamboo,
I do not recognize the soldiers
coming at me, it does not matter

that I know nothing, I have
never known anything, I see red fire—
the next time they are above me,

I am running across a field, a simple
moving target, red on green, I hear
a long whine, over and over I dream

footprints on my face, floral tattoos,
while across the hall my father
sleeps, groaning with, growing into

the same dreams, same dreams,
the ambush, the betrayal, aerial
surveillance, interrogation, and wakes

with no memory, cannot recall any wound
a Korean girl wore like a blood tattoo,
any child running across bamboo fields alone.

Patricia Monaghan

Of Accidents and Loss and War

He'd begged for the dog, so it was he who had to
feed it and walk it and, when it was killed, bury it.
He disappeared into the woods near the duck pond.
It was spring, the ground was hard, the grave took hours.
When he came back, it was done. He never mentioned it again.

Four years later, his friend's gun discharged during cleaning;
they ruled out suicide—he was an altar boy, daily communicant,
although why he was pointing a loaded gun at his head was
anyone's guess—and he locked himself in his room for three
days after the funeral, and never mentioned it again.

Later, when he joined the service, he liked to say there were
no accidents, everything was chosen, every man was clear about
everything he did, plane crashes were deliberate, war was part
of the pattern, the brave always survived. On the ruins of love
he built a theory: they'd chosen to die. He'd decided to live.

Patricia Monaghan

Now, In His Age, The Inner Sea

He drives up a narrow road along a cliff
above the sea, somehow he recognizes it,
this sea, somehow he knows this road, but

in Korea he would not be driving; he would
fly; he'd never see the place from such
an ordinary angle; he'd never be exposed, not

this way: bullets, bombs, rockets, all
at once explode beside him, behind him,
up ahead, force him off the road—into the sea—

The truck is flying, flying the air lit up
with fire all around, the sea opening a sudden
almond eye beneath him, he is flying

into the eye, he is being devoured by the sea—but
he was never on that road, he was in a different
danger, the choppy prop-sound, the round sound

of the brown earth cratering beneath his bombs,
the splatter sound of strafing and the ripping,
the shredding sound of aircraft fabric—no—

The truck falls from the cliff.
A green splash: the man drowning.
He tries to float: he tries to swim.

His efforts sap his strength. The sea swells.
It holds up and pulls down, both at once.
A huge wave aims the man towards shore.

Max Money

Max Money grew up in California's Napa Valley, graduated from Stanford University and joined the marines. He served as a platoon leader from 1951 to 1953. He retired from the Marine Corps Reserve as a Lt. Colonel in 1973. He is a member of the Guyer Barn Poets and the Poetry Society of Vermont. His first collection of poems Napa Valley Traces was published in 1991.

M. I. A.*

You don't think "freedom",
"human rights" or "police action"
when you're on the hill
and they're coming to take it.

"G. I.! Afraid, G. I. ?"

You think "Shit!" Dig in.
You fight
because you are here,
have the hot hand,
are fast with the clip.
Flares pop strobed light;
bugles, tracers witch the night.
Death comes on rubber soles.

Afterwards, the questions.
No one hears.
Other helmets come,
gather the fallen,
the broken M-1's, the BAR's.
No one finds you.
No one answers . . .

more

Max Money

Medals are sent home
with Escorted Letter
from the Army.

"We regret . . . "

The words tear her dreams
into sharp stones.
You remain on Hill 191
somewhere north of the Parallel,
the cause served. It causes
me to remember . . .

Yes, we *did* win.
The Truce holds.
You were a hero,
one of the heavy-duty men
who brought the world
together again.

* for Bob Jursch

Max Money

The Line Crosser*

Stealing the shadows and shrouding himself
the warrior moved slowly, silently
across the line to scout and return
with vital intelligence. "The Chief" was
cunning, resourceful and walked on the wind
honed to the craft by his Algonquian
elders before he left the degradation
of Cattaraugus reservation.

The enemy waited in the dark,
triggers at the ready, for sprung trip-wires,
slips of sound or flares of light. Death touched him
twice but could not hold him. The Chief always
completed his mission and was rewarded
with two Purple Hearts, a squad of his own
and promotion to sergeant, but not with
deliverance from totemic scars.

Swallowing the phantoms of slop-chute
elixir, the warrior sought relief
from life's sorties. Bitter whispers of
other enemies waited in the dark—
bigoted ethnic slurs that he had
never "fit". Bedeviled frequently by
dispirited stupors The Chief was busted
to private and discharged from the Corps.

The final battleground was far from
Korea—it lay in the septic wards
of Brooklyn's VA hospital where stealth
became death's pointman. But Chief was a
favored brave and in a silent blanket
the solitary warrior crossed the line
one more time and pulled permanent duty
in the sacred halls of Manitou.

* for Wilbur Shongo, U.S.M.C.

54

V. A. Hospital

The wounded sit like stones
creased by rivulets of time
slowly cracking within.
Outwardly, no sign.

Was a time they would buck
and rage and curse in streams.
No angry thunder now—
they sweat in fevered dreams.

On this plain of siege
All G.I.'s wait, forlorn,
the question unanswered.
Glory, far afield, torn.

Worn magazines lie unread,
doctors brush by in transit.
T.V.'s drone on unwatched.
Down the long hall, "Exit".

A reduced form rolls by
on a gurney and is gone—
no-man's-land—only the man
with the mop moves on.

Terry Moore

Terry Moore was a civilian for three years when, as a Reserve Officer, he was recalled for active duty in Korea as a Platoon Commander with The Royal Ulster Rifles. He was the only officer from his Rifle Company to escape from the Battle of the River Imjin. A Trustee of The British Korean Veterans Association, he is retired.

The Land of the Morning Calm

So this is the Land of the Morning Calm!
Is this the Land of the Free?
No! this is the land where my soldiers have died,
in search of your Liberty.

Liberty viewed from a prisoner's cell
Shines brighter than previously;
And here is the land where my comrades are chained,
Whilst searching for your liberty.

We were conceived in liberty;
Conceived in the Land of the Free,
But its here in the Land of the Morning Calm
We discharge our freedom for thee.

Rochelle Natt

Rochelle Natt has been published in <u>More Golden Apples</u>, <u>Pearl</u>, <u>Sojourner</u>, <u>Negative Capability</u>, and others. In 1991 she won honorable mention with the <u>Colorado Review</u>, and is the recipient of the Eve of St. Agnes Award and the Judah Magdes award. She lives in Great Neck, New York.

I'm Stuck Here on the Porch

Since Joe next door got polio,
his mother wails like Johnny Ray.
Dad stocked the bomb shelter.
Everyday Mom goes down there.
She made me stay on the porch.
"First F. D. R., now Joe," she warns.
Joe drags himself on silver crutches.
His legs have turned to sticks.
He and my cousin Lance used to run races.
Lance sent me a doll,
silk-pajamaed, china-faced.
Where's Korea anyway?
Nothing's the same anymore.
I'm stuck here on the porch.
The sky is covered with thick gauze.

Pat O'Connor

Pat O'Connor was a twenty-seven-year-old Canadian stretcher-bearer with the RCR when he was killed by Chinese machine-gun fire on the second-last day of May, 1951 while treating his comrades. This poem was found in his personal belongings. He was seen writing it the night before he was killed.

Korea

There is blood on the hills of Korea
Tis blood of the brave and the true
Where the 25th Brigade battled together
Under the banner of the Red White and blue
As they marched over the fields of Korea
To the hills where the enemy lay
They remembered the Brigadier's order:
These hills must be taken today
Forward they marched into battle ,
With faces unsmiling and stern
They knew as they charged the hillside
There were some who would never return
Some thought of their wives and mothers
Some thought of their sweethearts so fair
And some as they plodded and stumbled
Were reverentially whispering a prayer
There is blood on the hills of Korea
It's the gift of the freedom they love
May their names live in glory forever
And their souls rest in Heaven above.

Kathleen Patrick

Kathleen Patrick is a poet and fiction writer whose work appears in literary and commercial magazines including <u>We Speak for Peace</u>. She received a Loft-McKnight grant in poetry and was a finalist in the Mentor Series in both poetry and fiction. This poem is dedicated to her uncle, a U. S. Marine, who served in the Korean War.

Silk Dragons*

We sit in the kitchen,
fluorescent hum of midnight between us,
and talk around years of nameless sex,
screen doors left open and banging.
Jokes like slipcovers over everything.
I want to know why, but do not ask.
He wants to tell me.
He does not.

Family blames the war.
He came back a little less married.
Found out the first time
he looked at her, knew it was all over,
knew it wasn't.
I never knew her.
And something about chemicals in the war.
Rashes. I don't know; I was a child.
I remember a Korean jacket
covered with silk dragons,
their wild tails curling.

Smell of horse hair and sweat.
The coffee boils to nothing.
"But you have your life," I say.
"Give it a rest, Kate.
This ol' cowboy's dust.
I'm walking to Kansas City."
And he does as we sit there,
all night talking, together,
in the cream and sugar kitchen
and welcome him home.

* for Charles L. Smith

Gaston Pelletier

Dr. Gaston Pelletier, a native of Cohoes, New York, holds a degree in English from Siena College, New York, and the Doctor of Arts in English from the SUNY University Center at Albany. He served as Visiting Scholar at the University of North Carolina at Chapel Hill, at Cornell and Yale Universities. Currently he is Professor of English at the SUNY Technical College, New York. His work has appeared in numerous magazines and journals throughout the United States and Canada.

Remembering Roger

Hero, giant, far larger than life,
his was beyond some ordinary arm.
Thanks to his curve our Catholic
squad upset the Protestant bunch,
the fair-haired guys from the Y,
two of three, three out of five.
The high school coaches, public
and private, forever nosed about,
letting Roger's parents know how
good he was, how good he could be.
He was our ace, our stopper, star.
No, his was not some average arm.

Starting late (and twice kept back)
he was sixteen: more man than boy.
The nuns' favorite, he kept clean
the blackboards, windows, floors.
He had a way with girls, especially
with Rita, the sexton's daughter.
He took a year at the public high:
not only made the team, went six
and two, with a pair of shutouts.

more

Then out of nowhere came "Korea."
Rog upped up, soon was in the USMC.
What else could our hero-giant do?

After basic he showed off a stripe,
a marksman's medal, sunburnt face.
He pitched again in a pickup game:
couldn't touch him; he still had it.
A star, a giant—larger than life—
his could never be an ordinary arm.
He flew to camp; we walked to class.
He toted a rifle; we carried books.
He got it near the Yalu River—hit
in the shoulder by a sniper's fire.
When he got home the wing was gone.
Pinned to his chest: a purple token.

In due time our village was kind,
gave him a DAY, a hero's welcome.
Later, parading about our streets,
he (his sleeve) gathered attention,
but some, like Rita, recoiled, sure
that what was left would never hold.

Kenneth B. Perkins

Kenneth B. Perkins served nearly four years as a Hospitalman Second Class, two-and-a-half years on the Hospital Ship USS Haven. While in the Orient he became interested in poetry, particularly Haiku and Tanka.

U. S. S. Haven AH-12

Floating hospital—
Haven from the storms of war
For patients and crew.

All these years I've felt guilty
For having so safe a war.

Routine Admissions

All hands-flight quarters!
'Copter coming with five class
Able patients — plus.

Three orthopedics, one chest,
One head — and one for the morgue.

Monumental Dreams

No more monuments,
Nor solemn ceremonies
Bestowing medals.

No more young, mangled bodies
No more vain, misguided wars.

Thomas A. Phelan

Thomas A. Phelan was born in New York, and served in World War II and Korea. His military service includes the US Army Transportation Corps, US Navy Amphibious Forces, and US Marine Corps. He is a former detective with NYPD, and private detective. He is the author of A Point Beyond Silence, as well as many prize winning poems. He received the Golden Poet Award, New York Poetry Foundation Award, and International Poet of Merit. A novel, $6M Octopus, is currently at the publishers.

L'Espirit de L'Escalier de Korea
(A Testament which comes too late)

In the jungles of Korea, Marines, like
grotesquely broken and motionless puppets
that had fallen from their springs, died.
Others were going to die. A man screamed
to get away from the ground where he lay.
I was wild, yelled at the trees puncturing
the sky. Back home in a Naval hospital,
there were letters across my robe, M D U S A.
(Many Die, You Shall Also.)
In the burying grounds you can follow
granite stones of Brown, O'Reilly, Greenberg
and Diaz, to where my best buddy is buried.
All antiquity, a burying ground. I am
somebody lost in the wind, a frenzy, like
fire. Outside my window every morning the
birds make a ruckus in the quiet narrow
streets. In the face of civilized decorum
there my be hope for enlightenment.

Foster M. Phillips

Foster M. Phillips was born in Puebla, Mexico, the son and grandson of Presbyterian missionaries. In 1943 he enlisted in the US Marines and served in the South Pacific. He was commissioned after receiving his BA in political science from Yale University. During the Korean War he led a Marine rifle platoon and company. Later he received the M. Div and an MS in Bilingual Education, and is currently senior partner in InterAmerican Initiatives in Brewster, Massachusetts.

Friendly Fire

Huddled beside the upward path,
Heads down, bowed to dankness.
Distant cannons pound the fort
Shells roar by, a few yards up.

Pungent pine and moist earth smell,
Suspiring shattered branches,
Screeching shells blast hostile citadel,
Squinting men hold breath and shadow out the sun.

One rises, circle-sprays with rifle fire,
Vacant stare and foaming mouth,
Terror showers all around,
Friend and foe alike are sprayed.

Leader rises, slaps him hard;
Man explodes in teary rage.
Corpsman leads him down the hill,
Forever tinged with terror madness.

Foster M. Phillips

Line Through the Mark*

Gaze West across San Francisco Bay.
Lights twinkle dim on ocean waters.
Golden Gate wrapped in shrouds of fog.
Soft music weeps, permeates the room.

At seventeen, deceived by drama,
I'm more concerned at underage than any danger West.
At twenty-three I welcome in the sentiment,
Wrapping me in foggy shrouds of gloom.

Coming-homes are different too.
Eighteen screams for woman (any woman). . .
At twenty-five I yearn to hold my son.
My eyes searchlight the Eastern coast.

To West is massive death in moments on a beach.
Forever agony among the frozen hills.
To East is fecund life, creating babies,
Making love, making money, having fun.

Looking East across the LINE is living,
Why does looking West forever grip my mind?

* "Twice I've gone to war in the Pacific, (strange name) after saying
goodbye in the lounge atop the Mark Hopkins Hotel, San Francisco. Twice
I've come home and said hello again to life, in the same place. In my mind
there is a LINE through the center of that room separating dark from
light."

Foster M. Phillips

Tommy*

TOM

1. His mother and his father saw him off in Boston town.
They smiled and waved a flag as the tears rolled down.
His lady held her hand on the middle that would swell.
While Tommy's distant future no one now could tell.

CHORUS: Hey, hey, Tommy McVeigh,
       Who was the one that blew you away?
       Why did he do it? He didn't say,
       On that lovely autumn day.

2. On the rocky, rocky ridges in another generation,
Tom McVeigh died without any veneration.
There was nothing left to bury, no memorial to the man,
Only fleeting, longing images in our mind's scan.

CHORUS:

3. The man who pulled the lanyard never saw the man he slew.
Shall we hate the hand that did it? Was it me? Was it you?
Or his commanding officer who tried to send him back,
To tote his tiny baby in a bright red pack?

CHORUS:

*In December, 1950 1st Lt. Thomas McVeigh left Boston. He was assigned to B
Co., 1st Bn., 7th Marines, First Marine Division. He led a rifle platoon gallantly.
In September 1951 Tommy was "rotated to the rear" by his commanding officer.
Two days later he received a random Chinese artillery round, head on. There was
nothing left to bury. It was his son's first birthday.

Foster M. Phillips

November 10, 1951

Seventh Marines on ridge-line;
Across valley, mountain forts.
Chinese ants walk across skyline;
We see them observing us.

Regimental Colonel comes to line,
Cake passed out, a piece for each,
Colonel speaks, standing on knoll;
Marine Corps Birthday celebration!

He raises up his scimitar,
Ceremonial sword in air.
"To those who went before; to those who die!"
Cup lifted up, sword flashes down.

A hundred cannon roar behind,
Battleship rounds fly overhead.
Mortars join in, Chinese mountain explodes.
We eat our cake and watch the smoke.

Wilson M. Powell

Wilson M. Powell served in the USAF from 1950 to 1954. He was assigned in Taegu, as an Air Policeman, in September of 1952. He left, at age twenty-one, on the day the Armistice was signed. After semi-retirement he now lives in St. Louis, Missouri, where he works in hazardous materials management, and writes poetry.

The Eyes of Korea

I wanted to escape
the eyes of POWs
hunkered down
resting from filling sandbags
staring quiet hate at me.
I was afraid, dismayed
shakily indignant
what had I done to them?

The old man's eyes
told me nothing
as he stood under his huge
A-frame load of sticks
waiting for me to decide
if he was enemy or not.
Did he care? I couldn't tell.

The smiling prostitute's
wrinkles overran her face
without touching the eyes.

more

Wilson M. Powell

Contempt, brutality
hard-cored the
National Police Lieutenant's
otherwise artless eyes.
He liked our trucks
hated our drivers
pursued his graft in secret.
He gave me a big, big smile
after shooting his own
sleeping guard.

The eyes over the prisoner's
split, swollen cheekbones
flashed helpless rage
with each impact
of the Police Lieutenant's
gloved and weighted hand;
stoically dulled
at the questions in between
closed altogether
when he passed out.

A young soldier
killed his first enemy
then talked too much,
eyes convulsing
as fear and triumph
relief and shame
took turns battering his future.
The sergeant's eyes were tired
when he told him,
"The choice wasn't yours.
Forget it."

more

Wilson M. Powell

Another soldier's eyes looked within
at spectres unimaginable
as he tried to tear away his face
from shame, just shame.
My arms tired
holding his down all night
compassion stretched
from talking reason
to the unheeding ears,
of a casualty
who would receive no Purple Heart.

Two boys frozen together
in each other's arms.
I couldn't see the eyes
I knew were in there
looking at their last dreams.

One boy,
hands on stolen wood
to build his hut,
stood wide-eyed, paralysed
trembling until half way through
the heated C-ration.
Then he smiled
all the way up to his eyes.

The farmer's eyes,
humbly shadowed
under downcast brow,
were warmly grateful
shaming us who could only bring
money and things to support
his compassion for orphaned children.

I wanted his eyes to find mine.

Harold L. Putnam

Harold L. Putnam is married, and the father of two daughters and three granddaughters. A life long resident of Ithaca, Michigan, he entered the Army 1 November 1950 and served with the 9th Inf Regiment, 2nd Inf Division until January 1952. He is currently Director of Gratiot County Department of Veterans Affairs. He holds the CIB, National Defense Medal, United Nations Korean Service Medal with 4 stars, Presidential Unit Citation, and the ROK Presidential Unit Citation.

Ghosts of War

Fear stalking our senses
moving stealthily through the
hidden recesses of our mind
more terrifying than the reality
we faced in days long past
but dimly recalled
The fearless immortality of youth
replaced by the uncertainty of
mortality not acknowledged then
but lost by time
echoes echoes of the past
have reached us . . touched us
at last. . . at last.

Ron Rash

Ron Rash was born in 1953 and feels a link to the Korean War. An author-poet, he has published in the <u>Habersham Review</u>, is the winner of an NEA Poetry Fellowship for 1994, and has a book of short stories published by Bench Press.

A Korean War Veteran Nightfishes the Catawba River

The lantern's flame is a whisper.
This black night I drift blind
under the snuffed-out stars.
War teaches there is no silence.
the water's soft slap marks the shoreline.

I cast to that sound, the bank
where willow oaks bend over feeding bass,
and hear no splash but feel
the line tighten too high,
snagged in unseen branches.

I jerk at the dark and something
jerks back. My rod tip quivers.
I have caught the sky.
Something strains upward
like a soul trying for heaven.

A cautious man would break off.
I start reeling, bring it down,
into my almost-capsized boat
where the lantern lights a face
ugly enough to be human.

My rag-wrapped left hand stills
leathery wings. The right
risks six weeks of shots
freeing the barb, giving back
what belongs to the night.

A Korean War Veteran Nightfishes the Catawba River was first published in *The Habersham Review*.

Elisavietta Ritchie

Elisavietta Ritchie's <u>Flying Time: Stories & Half-Stories</u> includes four PEN Syndicated Fiction winners. Her poetry collections include <u>The Arc of the Storm</u> and <u>Elegy for the other Woman: new and selected terribly female poems</u>, <u>A Wound-Up Cat and Other Bedtime Stories</u>, and the award-winning <u>Raking the Snow</u>. Editor of <u>The Dolphin's Arc: Poems on Endangered Creatures of the Sea</u>, and other books, she lives in Toronto and Washington, DC.

Korean Landscape, 1977*

One plum tree
blooms again
beside the crater.

Patrols of pines
still bend and writhe
against a sky on fire.

Cranes and jets
fly through
the moon.

The landscape
has not
changed.

* for an estranged husband who photographed his battlefield in April, 1952.

Elspeth Cameron Ritchie

Major Elspeth Cameron Ritchie, MD was born in San Francisco, raised in Washington DC and currently lives in Silver Springs, Maryland. She wrote these poems in Korea, serving as the 2nd Infantry Division Psychiatrist. Currently she is stationed at Walter Reed Army Medical Center. These poems were first published in <u>Military Medicine</u>, the journal of the Association of Military Surgeons of the United States.

General Medical Officer, Camp Casey, Korea

Saturday, the PX is filled;
soldiers eat Anthony's pizza,
buy videos and lacquer boxes
for pregnant wives back home.

I ride to the East Casey gym,
pump iron, admire my growing arms,
compete with younger men and
wipe sweat from the vinyl bench.

Later the officer group goes
to the Second to None club
where a Korean dancer writhes
wearily to Credence Clearwater.

The men too are bored, waiting for
the trip to downrange, outside the gate.
There older women with flat faces
squat on the curb, pimping for
minishorted girls in the alleys.

Stalls line the road, sell soju,
fried squid and 2 ID t-shirts.
Vendor bargain with five fingers,
deaf since rubella-shrouded birth.

Shattering fantasy, a siren shrills.
Soldiers leave drinking, run to barracks,
throw on BDUs, lace combat boots,
brush teeth, race to the weapons room.

more

Elspeth Cameron Ritchie

They leave with M-16s, gas masks,
rucksacks, MOPP gear, candy bars,
to service HUM-Vs in the motor pool.

We doctors, useless, play cards,
or sleep, with rucks for pillows.
The work here is for fighting men
whose job is to train and wait.
Our job is to support and repair
broken heads, penile drips,
wrists slashed, men wanting home.

3:30 AM, alert over, we check our 45s.
But my beeper sounds: a man jumped
off the roof of his hooch. Soju
again. Sweet potato liquor.
I medevac him to Seoul.

Now dawn. Yellow lights still
outline the misted motor pool.
Faint rain hides tanks, quonset huts,
wreathes mountains which float to
North Korea. Our enemy seems remote.

Yet students throw firebombs.
There is movement north of the DMZ,
tanks clog the country roads,
and a crazy man overran Kuwait.

We also wait, drink OB beer,
sometimes pray, fear and
wish for Saudi sand and war.

We pass the time betting.

Elspeth Cameron Ritchie

Jewelweed

Hollow stems overstep my garden.
Weeds shade out begonias, lily bells.
Forgotten since their manic birth
pansies stretch weak stems,
velvet hearts arch towards shielded sun.

I yank out jewelweed.
Dirt embraces roots,
but resistance is weak.
The grass is tougher,
leaving foxholes where
a tattered mouse lies,
my cat's tribute abandoned.

This final weeding comes too soon.
I will be transplanted from summer
to the Cold War, Korea,
where tanks festoon gardens of graves,
guns overhang foreign flowers,
cooks serve dogs for lunch.

To pull up friendship is the hardest.
Some goodbyes are soft pops,
scars smoothed by rain.
Leaf bags line by time's curb.

Now my hoe catches on brambles.
Blackberry thorns
snag my heart as I leave,
and etch your name.

Elspeth Cameron Ritchie

Infantryman—the DMZ, Korea

Flame blue dress, black hair
to slim waist, spike heels.
A case of OB beer. Wrapped
in my poncho, I dream.

Pre-dawn, reveille:
platoon sergeant yells.
My toes are ice.
I pull on boots,
kevlar, M-16,
lie on the snow for
stand-to, point my
weapon at North Korea,
ponder girls and chow.

Bacon, eggs, weak coffee.
For lunch, an MRE.
Seven more nights of
churned mud. Once more,
no mail from home.

Shouts. A trac flipped,
crushing the head of
the leader of my squad.

In memorium:
three stacked rifles,
capped by his helmet,
boots shined blacker
than he ever wore.

more

Elspeth Cameron Ritchie

In dreary formation,
our sergeant calls roll.
Silence echoes his name.

He played third base,
would overthrow the ball
to me on first. I cursed
him last week when we lost.
Now taps.

I have his lucky mitt—
he courted his wife at
high school games—
and his March *Playboy*.
I seek our chaplain,
what should I do?
Send the mitt to his son,
throw away the porn.

Instead in garrison,
I lie on my bunk,
with the magazine,
pop a beer,
peer at white skin,
forever glossy
gleaming legs.

Our picture was in
The Indianhead,
as we learned to move,
shoot and communicate.
Grainy black and white.

more

Elspeth Cameron Ritchie

He sent copies home.
I brought my girl a paper.
she works at The Liberty Club.
We Texas two-stepped,
drank, made love.
Twenty thousand won.
Cheap to be a man.

Tonight, she doesn't come.
An officer?
I try to phone home;
all trunks are busy.
Country music wails
of loss and coffins.

How will I survive
training, lust, war,
my loneliness here?

The chaplain cannot answer,
for I dare not ask.

Mary Rutkovsky-Ruskin

Mary Rutkovsky-Ruskin's short stories have been published in <u>Cosmopolis:</u>
<u>Urban Stories by Women,</u> <u>Aegean Review,</u> <u>Caliban: The National Poetry</u>
<u>Magazine of the Lower East Side</u> and other anthologies and journals.
She currently resides in New York City and is working on a novel about
life in a single room occupancy hotel entitled <u>The Welfare Hotel.</u>

The Casualties of War

Father
don't leave me
with my waking dreams
of a war we both survived.
The 38th parallel still exists.
It is the line
mother and I cannot cross.
The gunfire is the
pain and emptiness I feel
when a male voice says the word goodbye.
The field mines are everywhere.
I never know when
I may take a step
that will strip my world to the bone.

Dad
don't leave me
all alone
with my teenage dreams of airplanes,
   bombs
    and mountain warfare.
I puzzle over the repetition
and detail of these dreams.
Relief arrived
years later
the day I read
that sensitive children
swallow whole
the unexpressed and painful experiences
of a parent.

more

Daddy
don't leave me
all alone
with three brothers
who shout louder
and demand more.
The three of us
alone with a momma gone mad.

Daddy
don't leave me
all alone
with the unknown.
I waited for your bedtime stories.
I imagined they would resemble
Uncle Alex's daring adventures
as a pilot.
But you were silent
when I was old enough
to not ask why.

Daddy,
don't leave me
all alone
in a land of
dirty diapers and unkempt rooms.
We are new in town
with no friends,
     neighbors
     or relatives to help.
We are three baby birds
with gapping mouths
screaming for the same worm.

more

Mary Rutkovsky-Ruskin

Father
forty years have passed.
I have devoured facts about the war.
Today
I ride a train home
to ask for your stories.

I need to hear more than,
"It was a horrible war,
you don't want to hear the details."
It is only by telling the stories
that you and I
will purge ourselves.
Memories and wounds
bind us together.
Casualties of war,
we have escaped
the statistician's eye,
wounded but unknown.

Father,
don't leave me
to uncover and tell the stories,
        dreams
            and nightmares
that you rightfully own.

Roy Scheele

Roy Scheele is an English teacher and Poet in Residence at Doane College in Nebraska. This poem is about growing up with the Korean Conflict as background. It was originally published in Pointing Out the Sky.

Playing at War

On the shady north side
of the house, beneath
my room's green windowscreen,
I kept a bank of dirt
packed loosely up against
the gray foundation blocks.

The conflict in Korea
directing me at play,
with front-page maps that showed
the Chinese sweeping down,
the fighting near Inchon,
I'd take my Army men

and build a hillside post,
a lonely mountain road,
holding out sleeplessly
against pajamaed hordes.
Then at the matinee
one Saturday I saw

Van Heflin starring in
The Steel Helmet. I knew
somehow it wasn't true,
only more make-believe,
and put my men away
till Dienbienphu.

Linda Jo Scott

Linda Jo Scott is Professor of English and Co-chairperson of the Department of Humanities at Olivet College, Michigan. She teaches literature and creative writing courses. In 1975 and 1976 she lived in Korea, and taught English Conversation at Dankuk University in Han Nam Dong.

Letter to A Korean Schoolgirl,
Written on A Bus in Seoul, 1975

My dear young lady,
Watching you give your seat to an old woman
Laden with cabbages in front, a grandchild on her back,
I can only smile with approval.

You look away shyly,
You in your straight-cropped hair,
Your gray school uniform,
Dark stockings and plain shoes,
A bundle of books on your back.

A quarter century ago, our fathers, grandfathers,
        brothers fought together for your freedom,
Yet you have lived all of your life in fear.
Perhaps you have family in the North whom you will never know.
Perhaps they themselves will plunder your city,
And you and your parents will try to cross the Han River to the South,
Knowing there will be too few bridges,
Too little time.

Korea, too, is a young school girl on a bus,
Serene, modest,
Jostled among the young and the old,
The cabbages and books,
The windows closed,
The order of Kimchi everywhere.

I would gladly offer you my seat here by the window
If I could even catch your black eyes.
Here in our crowded silence, younger sister,
I can offer only my prayer for our safe arrival,
For your freedom.

Louis Sinclair

Louis Sinclair lives in Waterville, Maine, where he is poetry editor for the Veterans for Peace Journal.

Inchon Morning

A wooden boat off-loads bags of rice
as women with small twig brushes
carefully sweep bouncing white grains,
forced out of the burlap weave,
on impact with the wooden dock,
into metal pans
which they then empty
cautiously into cloth bags
hung like small infants
at each woman's side.

Dark and distant mountains,
still rubble and scrub from shelling—
the poverty of picking limbs
for fuel, toys, digging implements
has left stripped skeletons of trees—
fear is still mirrored in faces.
Yesterday, a monk showed me a tunnel
where an ancient, thirty-foot Buddha
had been hidden during the war—
mushrooms grow there now in trays;
there is a clear rock-lined spring
in the corner of a small domed entrance
one wooden chair with a table and candle.

more

Louis Sinclair

I watch fishing boats
being towed to open water
while soft voices fade,
oil lanterns reflect orange
against the pink dawn sky
like a tongue on the tip
of the harbor's lip.

For a brief moment
the sweepers forget
I am American
and they are Korean;
all we see is people,
earth and sea,
together.

Constance M. Utley

Constance M. Utley currently lives in Lake Forest, Illinois. Her background is in art history and psychology. She writes children's stories and has recently returned to school at the University of Chicago. Her husband is a veteran of the Korean War.

Warrior

I follow his wounds from
Korean hills to Chicago.
Touching above his heart
my ligaments strain with the cold —
it's a frosty drum, empty of blood,
(red-red like a dove's warm breast).
His eyes of blue unfrozen water
weep at the song,
"Steal Away, Steal Away, Steal Away to Jesus."
It's just that he misplaced something.
A time of glory flowing like a stream,
where trees cast shade in a positive hour.
He knows *that* time, only for a time,
now there is nothing but
an age'd warrior binding himself
to the dusk.

William Wantling

*William Wantling was a man of "huge contrasts" said Len Fulton, his
publisher. He served in Korea, faced a season of heroin addiction, served
a period in prison, wrote, and faced life with a sort of Dostoyevsky
understanding. The poems here are from his book The Source.*

Korea 1953

Endless weeks of zero
A lurking bunker on a barren
     hill
Waiting to receive our orders
        Probe, Capture, Kill
As if one must recompense in
          limbo
For each probe which lacked
      all sense

In that strange war that was not
a war, that came to us too late
When we enjoyed sanctioned
     Murder
And sought the purge of murderous
          hate
We found a certain inner logic to
        our violence
A game in which each player and
    his mate
          understood all rules
(each sensing his brother's center)
And at expense of this -- genius of
        fools

William Wantling

    One might purge oneself
            so clean
    That love could come to our dead
            winter
                    for one cannot hold
                            an inner void
    And if one's hate is utterly
                    purged

    One's intuition told
            that love could enter
    And we, bold, would become merged
            with our idiot other selves
    And returned to time of childhood
                            Grace

    Yet we became
    as a pack of maddened dogs that race
            caged, snarling, for the hand
                    which flings
    The one small piece of rancid meat
    in the center of our corrupted sand
    . . . And the single victor cannot eat
    The prize before dying in his blood's
            slow-cooling heat.

William Wantling

Without Laying Claim

without laying claim
to an impossible innocence
I must tell you how
in the midst of that crowd
we calmly pulled the pins
from six grenades
mumbling an explanation
even we didn't believe
& released the spoons
a lump in our throats

The Korean

stood stiffly pressed against
    the wall
arms folded
        staring
. . . flinched
when the bullet sang
           fell
outward into the cobblestoned
    court
one too many holes in his head
for stealing from Americans

Keith Wilson

Keith Wilson is a native of Clovis, New Mexico. He entered the United States Naval Academy in 1945 and upon graduation served aboard the USS Valley Forge and later on the USS LST 1123 in Korea. He is Professor Emeritus at New Mexico State University in Las Cruces. He has published over twenty volumes of poetry including The Old Car and Other Black Poems, and Graves Registry.

Guerrilla Camp, Korea, 1952

We arrived at Sok To
before dawn, caught the last
of the tide & slipped the LST's bow
high on the beach.

> He was waiting, bent
> slightly over, hiding
> his hand. He didn't
> wave.

Later, after a good breakfast
aboard, an Army captain took
us on a tour of the guerrilla
camp:

> & he followed, tagged
> along like somebody's
> dog. A tall Korean,
> patient.

We were shown the kitchens, & the
tent barracks, the specially built
junks with their concealed engines

more

Keith Wilson

        & he watched, never
        leaving us with his
        eyes

Through the hospital, saw 4
sheetcovered bodies from the
raid the night before, didn't
ask whose men they were, spoke
kindly to the wounded & gave
them cigarettes

        until he strode up,
        stuck his shattered hand
        in my face, anger & hatred
        flaming in his eyes &
        shouted & shouted & shouted

        waving that hand, the
        bone crumpled by
        a rifle slug & pushed
        almost through the skin,
        hardened into a glistening
        knot

He was one of ours, a retired fighter,
about my age, my height. They told me
he wanted to know how a man
could farm
with a hand like that.

Keith Wilson

Old Times*

He is a veteran too
runs antique/junk shop he
takes out two thin bars of faded
campaign ribbons

                        WWII Service
United Nations Medal/Korean Service
(four battle stars) Occupation Medal,
Asian Clasp/Presidential Unit Citation/
U.S. Navy Citation/Korean Presidential
Unit Citation

Tom Breen and I both more than a little
drunk swaying through the streets of Sasebo
in a rickshaw, smokey fires, incense, the raw
air of winter in Japan. I buy my ribbons that
night because I am headed home, want to impress
my girl stateside. Can't remember anything
the next morning when I find them there on
my jacket's breast

star shell drifting down over our ship
& how I never can draw a breath until
it burns out for above the rumble of our
engines I can clearly hear the training
of coastal guns as they track our ship
through the winter night

                                        the
                    ghosts that still walk
                    the night whispering
                    the word   *"Korea"*

                                        more

Keith Wilson

"How much is it I ask?"

> *remembering the bodies*
> *swollen, floating in*
> *the Yellow Sea, my beard*
> *frozen, my eyes dead*
> *with exhaustion*

"Four Dollars," he says.
I pay him, he too from that forgotten war.
"Maybe you can let your grandchildren
play with these ribbons," he says.
His eyes hood, turn slightly away
towards whatever he sees in the exploding
shells ricocheting rounds that suddenly
fill the room, surround us both.

*for 1STSGT Robert L. Gaines, USMC

Keith Wilson

The Seventh Wave

In the aftermath of war it all swept around him.
The silence. No one mentioning where he's been.
He told a couple of people. "Korea," he said.
Both looked blankly, then grew embarrassed.

A younger friend, from Viet Nam, said later,
"Hell, at least they didn't spit on you!" He
couldn't say anything then, feeling the younger
man's pain too much to tell him silence
can be a way of spitting.

Years went by and he came to hate Veterans'
Day when "Korea" was never mentioned, or
briefly in passing. He would know one of his
own people was speaking then, nervously adding
this unmentionable war to the list of horrors.

"Did you know more people died in Korea
than in Nam? That it lasted longer?"
People smile uncomfortably wonder why
he is dragging up that old subject again.
He wonders, too, draws more into himself.

Trouble was, his bunch didn't organize,
felt, one guy said, like ghosts drifting
around a society who lived in news bites,
had no long-term memory at all, seeing all
wars as Desert Storms, made for TV. He said
he didn't care much anyway, we're almost
all dead now anyway, the Vet's Hospitals
closed by Reagan. "At last we get to die
our own way, by ourselves thinking of buddies
who didn't get the chance. Fuck 'em," he
said and walked away.

Keith Wilson

> "Anyone who has ever worn
> uniform should be declared
> a casualty . . . ."
> —Dorothy Thompson

War stories,

told around a mountain fire
by old men who almost touch their desire . . .
then sense they're fading, the moon, the skies

gently dimming their eyes,
they never see the darkened lead
grey woods silently fill with dead

who listen, nod their heads.
flinch at a snap from the fire, red
smoke trailing up, like a plane

falling down into flame.
"What were their names?" one asks
and the others shudder, dead, look past

cold meadows, where sacred datura
is in full bloom, the blood's own flora
making memory falter, dead, in the brain

until shadows take each other's hands, in pain
the files of wardead, bloodied to the bone
walk their paths, through nettles and stone,
sheaves and sheaves of war dead, each of us alone.

Denis J. Woods

Denis J. Woods, a Welshman, served two tours in Korea, with the South Wales Borderers, the Welch Regiment, and the Royal Artillery as a signals operator in a forward observation post. A former member of the governing body of the British Korean Veterans Association, he is well known for his eloquence, his poetry recitals and his deep Welsh baritone voice.

The Field of Crosses

The years have passed in plenty,
Since the time that I was there;
Along with countless others,
The burden for to share.

Now I often think of those who stayed,
Detained against their will,
'Neath a field of painted crosses,
On the side of a sun-baked hill.

What price the golden glory,
In the winning of the fight?
With you not here to share it,
But gone forever from our sight.

But you are not forgotten,
And this I remember, too,
But for the grace of God above,
I'd have shared that field with you.

Denis J. Woods

Before Endevours Fade

Let not their glory vanish
       with the setting of the sun.
       Let every generation
See their justice done!

They testify in silence
       From each known, and unknown grave.
       They did not live to witness
The world they fought to save.

Honour still, their memory,
       And each hasty promise made;
       That they might be remembered
Before endevours fade!

Ken Zellefrow

Ken Zellefrow grew up in western Pennsylvania. He spent four years with the Air Force, serving as a medic at K-16 outside Seoul during 1952. After discharge he completed his degree, receiving his doctorate from the University of Colorado. He taught English and composition for twenty-four years at New Mexico State University in Las Cruces. He has published in what he lists as "minor" journals. Dr. Zellefrow retired in 1992.

Ike

He came as he promised
Checked out the Marines
Because they were the ones winning the war
As always
Sailed through Seoul
Through ROK-lined streets
Keeping a promise to the folks
To see their boys were being treated right
Were winning
Were packing to come home for other wars
I don't know if he told them
They were dying
Keeping a promise he made sincerely
While his fellows, politicians,
Smiled knowingly and rubbed their hands.

Ken Zellefrow

Chosen

By whom?
This land of browns and greens
Dim and dusty and chilled
Smells where mainly Kimchee and paddies
Devastated places still holding a trace of order
Brown sluggish rivers
From which young kids pulled fish
Taking them someplace
Tails dragging in the dust.
No dogs
People squatting
The pose of subjugation
From the Khan to the Japanese to Rhee
The toilets survived
For they were flush to the earth
To accommodate the squatting.
Laborers in unison
Attacking a roadway
Picks lifted and dropped together
No one looking to see where he hit
This resilient earth which showed little
Sign of wear
Buses always crowded
People walking and bicycles and an occasional
Ox
People smiling, bobbing heads
Over tin pails of rice and something from a fish.
Patient people
Waiting for us to tire of saving them
And leave their land to them and time.

Glossary of Unfamiliar Terms

A-Frame: A wooden frame strapped to the back and used by the Koreans for carrying large loads.

Brens: A British .303 light machine gun used in Korea.

Bronze Star: A United States decoration awarded for heroic or meritorious achievement.

Chosin: The site of the Chinese intervention in which X Corps was trapped, and thus a symbol of the grand retreat of Army and Marine forces in the face of tremendous odds.

DMZ: Demilitarized Zone, line dividing Korea between North and South along which armed units guard the border.

Dum-Dums: A bullet cut so it will separate upon striking, increasing the damage of the wound.

Gook: GI slang for Korean, usually meaning North Korean.

Hootch: House

Howitzer: A field piece with a diameter greater than .30mm that drops its shell in an arc; 105s and 155s were most common in Korea.

Lanyard: Rope used for firing a field piece (howitzer).

Limmie: A British trooper in Korea.

MDUSA: Medical Department United States Army, printed on hospital gowns.

MP: Military Police

M-1: United States, .30 semi-automatic, gas operated, clip fed rifle, the primary weapon of the infantryman in Korea

M-1: United States, .30 semi-automatic, gas operated, clip fed carbine, used by officers and artillerymen in Korea.

M-16: Automatic rifle.

Naffe House: British canteen in Korea, name used to represent anyplace to get coffee and relax.

Number One: Slang phrase for "the most" meaning either best or worst.

Number Ten: Slang phrase for "the worst" or "way out."

105s: 105 MM howitzers

155s: 155 MM howitzers

PX: Post Exchange, usually meaning any government operated store.

POW: Prisoner of War

Purple Heart: United States decoration awarded for wounds.

Quad .50s: Truck mounted four .50 caliber machine guns used against light planes and massed troops.

Recon: Reconnaissance patrol.

Retread: Veteran of World War II called back in for the Korean War.

ROK: Republic of Korea, also, member of the army of the Republic of Korea.

Shitdiggers: British name for their infantry.

Short-timer: Someone with only a short time left before rotation home.

USMC: United States Marine Corps

UN: United Nations

Vickers: British .303 medium machine gun used in Korea.

Whirleybird: Helicopter

Zip (Zippo): Cigarette lighter famous during World War II and Korea for working in the wind.

Center for the Study of the Korean War

The Center for the Study of the Korean War is a foundation dedicated to the preservation of the individual artifacts of the veterans of the Korean War. The Group is interested in the accession and care of historical items, the collection of documentary and secondary materials, and the sponsoring of historical interest in the Korean War. The Center is incorporated as a not-for-profit organization in the state of Missouri, with tax exempt status granted by the IRS.

The Korean War has long been considered America's forgotten War. Today, after forty years of neglect, the facts of the War are slowly beginning to come to emerge, and growing as an area of interest in the American conscience. Now, nearly half-a-century after the Korean War began America is talking about a monument to those who fought and died there. It is the primary mission of the Center to encourage knowledge about the Korean War and its veterans.

The Center office, housing the library and archives, is located on Main Street on the Square of historic Independence, Missouri. The Center is served by an Director, Executive Secretary, and interested volunteers under the guidance of a Board consisting of veterans, librarians, archivists, and historians.

Not a veterans organization itself, the Center is friendly and supportive of, but not associated with, either the Korean War Veterans Association nor any of the unit associations or reunion groups. Rather it is a center for the collection of materials, and serious scholarly inquiry into the nature of the War, as well as the preparation of historical and educational materials. Its primary purpose is to encourage the study of the Korean War, and to push for a greater understanding and appreciation of the military and political issues at stake.

In addition to collecting materials concerning the war, and publicizing the war as widely as possible, the Center is interested in compiling bibliographic tools. Among those are General Matthew B. Ridgway: An Annotated Bibliography (1993) and The Pusan Perimeter, Korea: 1950-1953 (1993) The Inchon Landing, Korea, 1950 (1994) all published by Greenwood Press. The Hermit Kingdom, a book of poetry from the Korean War, is the most recent.

Those interested in association with the Center are urged to write to the Executive Director, Center for the Study of the Korean War, P. O. Box 456, Independence, Missouri, 64051.